HOW SHOULD TEENS
READ THE BIBLE?

✘CULTIVATING BIBLICAL GODLINESS

Series Editors

Joel R. Beeke and Ryan M. McGraw

Dr. D. Martyn Lloyd-Jones once said that what the church needs to do most of all is "to begin herself to live the Christian life. If she did that, men and women would be crowding into our buildings. They would say, 'What is the secret of this?'" As Christians, one of our greatest needs is for the Spirit of God to cultivate biblical godliness in us in order to put the beauty of Christ on display through us, all to the glory of the triune God. With this goal in mind, this series of booklets treats matters vital to Christian experience at a basic level. Each booklet addresses a specific question in order to inform the mind, warm the affections, and transform the whole person by the Spirit's grace, so that the church may adorn the doctrine of God our Savior in all things.

HOW SHOULD TEENS
READ THE BIBLE?

JOEL R. BEEKE

REFORMATION HERITAGE BOOKS
GRAND RAPIDS, MICHIGAN

How Should Teens Read the Bible?
© 2014 by Joel R. Beeke

Reformation Heritage Books
2965 Leonard St. NE
Grand Rapids, MI 49525
616-977-0889 / Fax 616-285-3246
orders@heritagebooks.org
www.heritagebooks.org

Printed in the United States of America
18 19 20 21 22 23/10 9 8 7 6 5 4 3 2

ISBN 978-1-60178-302-8

For additional Reformed literature, request a free book list from Reformation Heritage Books at the above regular or e-mail address.

HOW SHOULD TEENS
READ THE BIBLE?

If you had to make a list of things that characterize the Christian life, what would you include? I assume that grace would be high on the list. Christian lives should be gracious lives. Christians are people who have found peace with God through Jesus by grace alone, and their lives should radiate grace toward others. It is a characteristic that affects every area of their lives.

But what about simpler and more day-to-day things? I'm sure you could think of many things that Christians regularly do, but praying and reading the Bible would probably come to mind first. Praying and reading the Bible are things that Christians do all the time.

In this booklet, we're going to look at the second of those two things: reading the Bible. In particular, we will look at the Christian's daily reading of God's Word. But before we look at the very practical aspects of reading a Bible, we should settle two simple truths. The first is this: reading the Bible is hard work. The second is this: reading the Bible is totally worth it. If you keep these two truths in mind, you will save yourself from a lot of difficulty when it comes to reading the Bible. It's hard work, but it's worth it.

Most of you probably already know that reading the Bible is hard work. I'm sure you've tried and found it very difficult at times. Perhaps sometimes you've even given up. It might surprise you to know that reading the Bible is often hard work even for ministers. Sometimes I just can't wait for my next opportunity to read the Word of God, but that's not always the case. We're going to look at ways to make it easier and to find great joy in it, but that won't change the fact that it's hard work. If you are going to read your Bible seriously every day, you had better realize that you are in for some struggle. If you think it's going to be a relaxing walk in the park, you're going to be dreadfully disappointed. It's tough slogging, even for ministers.

WHY READING THE BIBLE IS HARD WORK

Why is it so tough to read the Bible? Here are three big reasons:

- The Bible is big. In fact, it's huge! It's more like a library than a book. It is a library of books: sixty-six of them. That's a lot of books! Some of you may not even own sixty-six books. The Bible I was using when I was writing this has some study notes at the bottom of the page, so it's a bit longer than many Bibles—just over two thousand pages! Even the average pew Bible has more than one thousand pages. The Bible is probably one of the longest books in your house. No wonder it's hard to read! It's long.

• The Bible has a lot of parts that are hard to understand. In fact, the apostle Peter admitted that he found some of what Paul wrote difficult to understand. So you're not the only one who's often left wondering what something in the Bible means.

• The Bible often seems irrelevant. Have you ever tried to read the first half of Isaiah, only to find pages and pages of curses against people with unpronounceable names who died thousands of years ago? What does that have to do with anything today? If the Bible is the biggest book you own and one of the most difficult books you've ever read, you need a good reason to go to all the work of trying to get through the whole book. If it seems irrelevant, you're unlikely to read it from cover to cover.

REASONS FOR READING THE BIBLE

So what reason could there be to read the Bible? Well, praise God, there are some very *good* reasons for reading this long, challenging book. Let me mention just three of them.

Read because It Is God's Word

First, we need to understand that the Bible is not irrelevant. In fact, it is the most relevant book ever written! It matters, and it matters a lot. Why? Because it is the Word of God to us. That is the biggest reason to read the Bible. It is the Word of God.

Now, you've probably heard that phrase—"the Word of God"—many times, and it may not seem all that important to you anymore. But think about it for a second. This book is God talking to us. This is God's message to His church. That's amazing! That's the biggest reason to read the Bible. Suddenly, the length of the Bible is a blessing! Praise God for giving us so much of His Word! What a treasure!

If you get an email from a friend you really like, you aren't disappointed if it's long, are you? The longer the better! When I'm travelling, I love to get long emails from my wife—the longer the better, because I love her. If you see an email in your inbox from someone you're really eager to hear from, you're terribly disappointed if you open it and it's only one line: "Sorry, I'm going away for a week; will write when I get back." That email is easy to read, but it leaves you wishing it were a lot longer! It would take more time and it definitely would be more work to read a longer email, but that extra work would be a pleasure, wouldn't it? The Bible is like a giant email from God to His church. It would be a lot easier to read if it was shorter, but who would want it to be! So that's the first reason and the greatest reason to read the Bible: it's a message from God.

Read for Truth

Second, the Bible is true. There are a lot of things in this life that are uncertain. People tell you things, and you're not always sure whether they are true. But the Bible is God's Word. God is truth; thus, His Word is true. Maybe one of your friends has lied to you. You thought you could trust him or her, but you've found out that you can't. You will find that much of life is like that. There are many things that you can't be totally sure about—ranging from what the media tells you to what friends tell you. People lie to me every day in emails from all over the world, telling me that if I provide certain information and follow their conditions, I can inherit millions of dollars. But all they want is to get information about me so that they can use me. They don't want to make me rich; they want to get richer off of me.

Truth is hard to find in today's world, but there is one place where we can be sure to find it: God's Word. God cannot lie, so whatever He says is true. That's a good reason to read the Bible. Charles Spurgeon, a famous English preacher from the 1800s, wrote: "The deeper you dig into Scripture, the more you find that it is a great abyss of truth" (*Complete Gathered Gold*, 60). In a world of shifting sand, God's

Word is rock solid. Stand there, build there, and you'll be safe. There's no doubt about it.

Read for Wisdom

Third, the Bible is full of wisdom—wisdom, first of all, for salvation. The Bible itself says that it is able to make you "wise unto salvation." Paul writes to Timothy: "From a child thou hast known the holy scriptures, which are able to make thee wise unto salvation through faith which is in Christ Jesus" (2 Tim. 3:15). The Holy Spirit has used the reading and studying of the Bible in the lives of countless millions to show them their sin, to drive them to Jesus Christ for salvation, and to train them to live the Christian life. He can grant you this wisdom, too.

But the Bible is also full of wisdom for practical daily living. When you run into situations where you're not sure what to do next, you might ask someone for advice—a friend perhaps. The advice your friend gives you may be very well intentioned; he or she might really and genuinely have your best interests at heart. But the advice could still be terrible. It might be very foolish. Your friend might have good intentions but lack wisdom. God never lacks wisdom, and His Word is full of it. There you will find principles to guide you that are both well intentioned *and* wise. You never have to wonder about the Bible's advice. It is the wisdom of God.

So those are three big reasons for reading the Bible. I'm sure you could think of more, but these three are very important and provide us with motivation to pick up the biggest book in our libraries and read it—it's from God, it's true, and it's full of wisdom.

PRACTICAL HELPS FOR READING THE BIBLE

But if we are going to be successful in attempting to read the Bible, we must discipline ourselves. Lots of people have had good intentions for reading the Bible but have ultimately given up on it. Maybe you're one of them. Perhaps the reasons we just went over for reading the Bible really excite you. But that excitement will soon wear thin when you start the difficult work of actually doing it. You have to be prepared for your enthusiasm to fade, and you have to be prepared for the times when you don't particularly *feel* like reading the Bible.

A football coach tries to think of all the plays the other team could be running and arranges his players in a formation that he thinks will best be able to stop the other team's play. In other words, he anticipates what the competition will do and sets up his team so that it won't be totally unprepared when the play starts. The same principle applies to getting ready to read the Bible. There is a lot of competition for your time and energy, and if you are going to get anywhere in your Bible reading, you have to step onto the field ready for the competition.

Arching over all of these preparations is God's grace. We need God's grace if we are to make any progress in Bible reading, and we certainly need it if we are going to benefit from our reading. You see, reading the Bible isn't a goal in itself; the goal is communion with God. If reading the Bible doesn't bring you into communion with God, then it's a failure. The goal is communion, not completing a checklist of passages read. And that takes grace. But the Bible itself is a channel of grace! It's a blessed circular system. You need grace for reading the Word, but grace comes through the Word. So get into the Word!

Grace is primary, but there are some very practical things you can do to help yourself read the Bible regularly and profitably.

Commit to a Time

The first and most important thing to do is to set a time. There are so many things that we have to do and so many things that we like to do that, unless we plan carefully, we'll never have any time left for reading our Bibles. So we need to plan. If reading the Bible is at the bottom of our priority lists, if we plan to do that after we've done everything else, we won't do it at all. If we don't set aside a time when we allow nothing else to intrude, we will not read our Bibles. It simply will not happen; hit-and-run Bible reading will become hit-and-miss Bible reading. Think about your day and pick a time for reading your Bible. Read your Bible at that time and don't let anything else crowd into it.

Find a Place

The second thing to do is to think of the best place to read your Bible, a place with no distractions. Don't try to read your Bible while sitting next to your brother when he is playing a video game. It won't work; you'll be hopelessly distracted. Your bedroom is probably a good place, especially if you have a room to yourself, but it's a bad idea to lie in bed while reading your Bible. That's a good position for falling asleep, but it's a terrible position for reading God's Word. You'll do more sleeping than reading. So find a good place and make it your regular spot for reading the Bible. If you make it a routine, your mind will automatically get into reading mode when you go to your reading place. If you do it somewhere different every day, you'll probably get distracted by new sights and sounds. So set a time and set a place. Take a second to think of a good place for reading your Bible.

Develop a Plan

Third, set a plan. A reading plan helps you know what you've read and what you haven't. Just randomly flipping open your Bible every day is a bad idea. There will be many portions of Scripture that you will never read. If you have no plan and you're wondering what to read one day, how likely are you to flip to Lamentations or 3 John? Not very. But if you don't read all the parts of the Bible, you will never develop a sense for its grand, overarching story.

There are lots of Bible-reading plans you can use, but a good one to start out with is a plan that takes you through the entire Bible in a year. A through-the-Bible plan makes sure that you read every part of Scripture.

Did you know that you can read through the entire Bible in one year by spending only fifteen minutes reading each day? There are 1,440 minutes in one day. If you use only fifteen of those minutes every day to read the Bible, which is about 1 percent of your time, you can read through the whole Word of God in one year. So plan your Bible reading. You'll never have to wonder what to read next, you'll always know what you've read and what you haven't, and soon you'll know that you've read the whole Bible. Some days, those fifteen short minutes will seem like a long time, but at the end of the year, when you've completed a one-thousand-page book, you'll see that reading the Bible in a systematic way isn't quite as hard as you thought it was.

How to Read
Scripture teaches us that the Bible must be read publicly in worship (Acts 15:21; 1 Tim. 4:13), but that it also serves as a blessing when personally read, heard, and obeyed. Revelation 1:3 says, "Blessed is he that readeth, and they that hear the words of this prophecy, and keep those things which are written therein."

But how should we read? One of the most helpful little books on reading the Scriptures was penned by the Puritan Richard Greenham (ca. 1535–1594), titled *A Profitable Treatise, Containing a Direction for the Reading and Understanding of the Holy Scriptures*. After establishing that the preaching and reading of God's Word are inseparably joined together by God in the work of the believer's salvation, Greenham focuses on our duty to read the Scriptures regularly and privately, gleaning support from Deuteronomy 6:6 and 11:18; Nehemiah 8:8; Psalm 1:2; Acts 15:21; and 2 Peter 1:19.

Becoming more practical, Greenham says that people sin not only when they neglect to read the Scriptures, but also when they read the Bible wrongly. He then gives us eights helps for how to read the Bible, each of which can be summarized in one word. Here they are:

1. *Diligence.* We must pursue diligence in reading the Scriptures more than in doing anything secular. We ought to read and study our Bibles with more diligence than men dig for hidden treasure, Greenham says. Diligence makes rough places plain; makes the difficult easy; makes the unsavory tasty. "Leave not off reading the Bible," Thomas Watson, also a Puritan, adds, "till you find your hearts warmed. Let it not only inform you but inflame you" (*Complete Gathered Gold*, 63).

2. *Wisdom.* We must use wisdom in the choice of mat-

ter, order, and time. Though we must read all of the Bible, as we have seen, it is not wise to spend most of our reading time on the hardest parts of Scripture. In terms of order, Greenham agrees that we should have a system that helps us get through the whole Bible, since only a whole Bible will make a whole Christian. As for time, no day should pass without reading the Bible. In fact, Greenham recommends that we read Scripture two or three times each day and at greater length on the Sabbath, because that whole day is devoted to worship.

3. *Preparation.* Proper preparation is critical. Without it, Scripture reading is seldom blessed. Preparation involves three things. First, we must approach Scripture with reverence, determined like Mary to lay up God's Word in our hearts (Luke 2:19). Second, we must approach Scripture with faith in Christ, looking to Him as the Messiah who can open our hearts just as He did for the disciples traveling to Emmaus (Luke 24:27). Third, we must approach Scripture with a sincere desire in our hearts to be taught by God (Prov. 17:16) and with a longing to study it in detail. The great sixteenth-century church Reformer Martin Luther said he studied the Bible in the same way he gathered apples: "First, I shake the whole tree that the ripest may fall. Then I shake each limb, and when I have shaken each limb I shake each branch and every twig. Then I look under every leaf" (*Complete Gathered Gold*, 60).

4. *Meditation.* Read slowly, thoughtfully, and meditatively. Some portions of Scripture—the book of Proverbs, for example—need to be read extra slowly in order to allow time for meditating on each verse. It is better to read five verses from Proverbs with meditation and prayer than one hundred without them.

Meditating on what we read in the Bible is critical. "Meditate on the Word in the Word," said Puritan John Owen (*Complete Gathered Gold*, 61). You can read diligently, but the reading will bear no fruit if you don't stop to think about and study what you have read. Reading may give you some breadth of knowledge, but only meditation and study will give you depth. The difference between reading and meditation is like the difference between drifting and rowing toward a destination in a boat. If you only read, you will drift aimlessly; if you meditate and pray over what you read, you will have oars that will propel you to your destination.

One helpful way to increase your meditation on the Bible is to memorize one verse each day from your Bible reading. Meditate on that verse throughout the day as much as you can. This is particularly important when you are young. Most of the verses that I have in my memory today are ones I memorized as a teenager. Fill your minds with Scripture now, dear young people, and it will benefit you for your entire life.

5. *Fellowship.* Greenham actually calls this "conference," but he means that you should fellowship with others about what you read in the Bible. You should especially talk with other believers about the truths of the Bible. That will help you grow in knowledge. Proverbs 27:17 says it this way: "Iron sharpeneth iron; so a man sharpeneth the countenance of his friend."

6. *Faith.* Our Scripture reading must be mixed with faith. Faith is the key to getting real profit from reading the Bible (Heb. 4:2); without it, it is impossible to please God (Heb. 11:6). "To read without faith is to walk in darkness," said Luther. It is to read in vain. By faith, as Scottish minister and hymn writer Horatius Bonar said, "we must not only lay the Bible up within us, but transfuse it through the whole texture of the soul" (*Complete Gathered Gold*, 59).

7. *Practice.* The fruit of faith must be practice; the read Word must be done. Dr. Martyn Lloyd-Jones, a well-respected Welsh preacher of the twentieth century, wrote: "It is a good thing to be a student of the Word, but only in order to be a practiser and experiencer of the Word" (*Complete Gathered Gold*, 60).

We must read the Word with the goal of obeying it. We must prayerfully aim for believing obedience, willing obedience, submissive obedience, loving obedience, wholehearted obedience, prayerful obedience, dependent obedience, and childlike obedience. The more we put the Word into practice in the daily obedience of faith, the more God will increase our gifts for His service and for additional practice. When the Spirit sheds light upon our conscience that we are "doing" the read Word, we also receive the great benefit of being assured that we possess faith.

This means that we must examine ourselves by what we read. For example, if you read Proverbs 3:5, "Trust in the LORD with all thine heart; and lean not unto thine own understanding," pause to ask yourself this: Am I, by grace, trusting in the Lord? What areas of my life am I not surrendering to Him? In what areas am I not putting this text into practice, but, instead, leaning to my own understanding? Then repent of these things, and turn to God in prayer for forgiveness and for strength to change.

8. *Prayer.* Prayer is essential throughout our reading of Scripture, for we are dependent on the Holy Spirit to enlighten us, to give us understanding, and to apply the Word to our souls and lives. Pray before you read the Bible, while you read it, and after you read it. In public reading of Scripture, it is not possible to pause and pray after each verse. In private reading, feel free to salt Scripture constantly with short, pungent, applicable petitions suggested by the particular verses being considered.

If we pray for nourishment from our physical food at every meal, shouldn't we pray much more for spiritual nourishment from every Bible reading? If we do not dare touch our food and drink before we pray, how do we dare touch God's holy Book—our spiritual food and drink—without prayer?

If the Bible is to get into us, we must get into it. Charles Spurgeon said, "Backsliders begin with dusty Bibles and end with filthy garments" (*Complete Gathered Gold*, 62). To neglect the Word is to neglect the Lord, but those who read Scripture "as a love-letter sent to you from God," as Thomas Watson put it, will profit from it. "Think in every line you read that God is speaking to you," Watson went on to say; then, by the Spirit's enlightening, you will experience its warming and transforming power.

Read and study the Bible to be wise; believe it to be safe; practice it to be holy. Lay hold of it until it lays hold of you.

PRACTICAL HELPS FOR STUDYING THE BIBLE

I've already implied that your reading of the Bible will be greatly enhanced if you study the Bible as you read it. But how should you study it? Here are a few helpful hints.

Study One Book of the Bible at a Time

Here are some suggestions: (1) Get a good book, such as William Hendriksen's *Survey of the Bible*, which presents introductory material on each Bible book, showing you its major themes, purposes, and outline. Read this first. (2) Read straight through the Bible book without looking back at your introductory volume. (3) Read the Bible book again, this time reading it along with the introductory volume, until you have a good grasp of the book's outline, flow, and themes. (4) Ask yourself questions like these: Are there words or phrases that keep reappearing? What do they mean? For example, in Ephesians you notice the frequency of the phrase "in Christ"; in Philippians, it is the word *joy*. (5) Read the book once more, using Bible study notes on the bottom of the page. As you read the text and the notes together, apply what you are discovering to your own heart and life. Returning to Philippians for a moment, you cannot help but notice that Paul has great joy even as he writes this epistle from prison. The message is clear: true Christians can triumph over adversity. Ask yourself: Am I doing that right now in my life? How could I do it better? (6) Read through the Bible book once more, this time with a few good commentaries by your side, or perhaps a series of sermons (Lloyd-Jones would be great on Philippians), and go slowly, prayerfully, and meditatively. Use John Calvin's, Matthew Henry's, and Matthew Poole's commentaries on the whole Bible; Calvin's and Henry's commentaries can be found online at the *Christian Classics Ethereal Library* (www.ccel.org), and Poole's commentary is available as a free Google ebook. You should also consider purchasing the best commentaries on individual Bible books that your financial means will allow. They can be of great help to you. (7) Speak to others about your study or, better yet, join a Bible study group that is seriously studying this book.

Study One Chapter at a Time
Here are ten questions to ask of every chapter of Scripture:

1. *What does this chapter teach me about God?* Look for teaching about His attributes, attitudes, and actions.

2. *Specifically, what does this chapter reveal about Christ?* Look for Christ in all the Scriptures, including the Old Testament. He is the key to, and the message of, the entire Bible (Acts 10:43).

3. *What doctrines are taught in this chapter?* Make a list of them with relevant quotations from the chapter and any cross references you may know.

4. *Who are the leading characters?*

5. *What are the main events?*

6. *What sins and follies are stated or implied?* Examine your heart in the light of this list. Which things in the list, or suggested by it, do you need to confess and forsake?

7. *What are the virtues evidenced in this chapter that I should seek after and cultivate?*

8. *What new thing have I seen and what old truth has the Lord brought with fresh blessing to my heart?*

9. *What are the key words and phrases that call for further study?*

10. *Which one thing may I remember this chapter by?* (adapted from "10 Commandments of Bible Study")

Study Individual Words and Verses
We grow in depth in our Bible study when we look carefully at individual words and verses in their biblical context. Assuming you have not studied Old Testament Hebrew or New Testament Greek, the best way you can do this is by purchasing three books: *Strong's Concordance; Theological Wordbook of the Old Testament (TWOT)* by Harris, Archer, and Waltke; and *Vine's Expository Dictionary of Biblical Words.* Begin by looking up key words of a text in *Strong's*, then use the number just to the right of the word entry to look up the fuller meaning of that word in the back, as well as in *TWOT* for Old Testament words and in *Vine's* for New Testament words.

Then make a list of the word in its contexts. Study the contexts for clues to its meaning. Find clear passages to illustrate the senses you have seen in the word. This may seem a bit tedious at first, but if you persist, you will soon find it stimulating and exciting.

As you study, ask questions. Given the meaning of these words, what is the text saying? What is God's particular message in this particular verse located in this particular chapter? What is the doctrine being explained? What experience of believers is being opened up?

Study Various Subjects in the Bible

There are thousands of exciting subjects to study in the Bible. Many of them are doctrines—such as the sovereignty of God or the intercession of Christ. Others are practical topics, such as how Christians should cope with suffering. Or you might want to study an individual Bible character, such as Noah, Elijah, or Peter. Above all, don't forget to make Jesus Christ, the Living Word, your supreme object of study. Study Christ in His person, offices, states, natures, and benefits. Study His character. Study His parables and miracles.

Thousands of biblically sound Reformed books are now available to help you study in all these areas and tens of thousands more. Get a list from Reformation Heritage Books in Grand Rapids, Michigan, and begin to read solid Reformed literature, if you are not doing so already, in conjunction with your Bible study.

Study the Basics of Sound Principles on How to Interpret the Bible

I highly recommend that you read chapters 3 and 4 of R. C. Sproul's *Knowing Scripture*. You will find those chapters simple to understand and extremely helpful. Let Sproul teach you how to compare Scripture with Scripture, how and when to take the Bible literally, what methods of interpretation to use for various genres of Scripture, and so much more.

Study the Personal Life Applications That Flow from the Text

Given your background, your circumstances, and your challenges, ask yourself these questions: What are these particular words and this particular verse saying to me in a practical way today? What is the practical truth I can apply to my own life here? Can I grow in my knowledge of a particular doctrine from this verse? Does the study of this verse prompt me to see some guidance for my daily life—perhaps something to be thankful for or some change that must be made, by the strength of the Spirit? Is there some sin exposed here that I must fight more earnestly, some righteousness that I must pursue more aggressively, some promise that I must embrace more fully? What should I experience from studying this verse? How should I feel concerning this passage? Should I respond with joy, sorrow, or a mixture of the two?

Study to Avoid Pitfalls That Result from Reading Scripture in an Imbalanced Way

Don't read too fast. Don't read without praying. Don't read just to fill your mind with truth. Don't be proud of what you know.

Don't be too discouraged if you fail to read the Bible rightly in many ways. Don't give up. Ask for forgiveness and start reading afresh. Let the Word fill your head, soften your heart, and move your hands into action. There you have it—head, heart, and hands. Let your Bible reading impact your entire life.

We've seen some really important reasons to read the Bible, and we've looked at some tips to help us get that reading done and study what we read. If you follow this advice, I pray that you will discover that reading the Bible is not a burden or only a duty that we have to get through so we don't feel bad about ourselves. Reading the Bible can be an experience full of joy and delight. It can be the best time of your day.

THE JOY OF READING THE BIBLE

We're going to conclude by looking at the joy of reading God's Word. But before we get to specifics, we have to establish one very important thing. Without understanding this truth, you will never have any joy in reading the Bible. This is the most important part of this booklet. Reading the Bible will *not* save you. In fact, reading the Bible won't change the way God looks at you at all.

If you are an unbeliever, reading your Bible, in itself, will get you no closer to God. Don't think that you can feel a little bit safer on days when you've read your Bible. You can't. And if you are a believer, reading the Bible will not make you any more acceptable or pleasing in God's sight. Not reading your Bible will not make you any less acceptable or pleasing in His sight. The difference between a believer and an unbeliever is Jesus Christ; it's grace, and nothing else.

Until you see that reading your Bible gets you no points with God, you will never be able to enjoy it. Why? Because you will always fail in reading it. You will fail to read it as often as you should; you will fail to read it as carefully as you should; you will fail to understand its meaning; and you will fail to see its wonder. You will fail again and again. So if you are hoping that your Bible-reading performance is earning you points with God, you are going to be one of the most miserable people on earth. You will be constantly losing points and losing heart until you finally give up in despair and quit reading the Bible altogether.

But the good news of the gospel—the good news of this book you're trying to read—is that you don't have to earn God's favor by reading your Bible. Jesus Christ and His righteousness is the only way to God, and unless you are trusting in Him for *all* your forgiveness and *all* your acceptability with God, you will never find joy in reading your Bible. So turn to Him; trust in Him and come see the joy that can be found in reading the Word of the Lord, the Word of Jesus, the Savior.

In the Bible itself, we find a record of those who loved God's Word and found great joy in it. The Psalms in particular are full of expressions of this joy: "I will delight myself in thy commandments, which I have loved" (Ps. 119:47); "I delight in thy law" (Ps. 119:70b); "I rejoice at thy word, as one that findeth great spoil" (Ps. 119:162). Jeremiah has this to say: "Thy words were found, and I did eat them; and thy word was unto me the joy and rejoicing of mine heart" (Jer. 15:16a). These men tasted the grace of God and loved God's Word.

Throughout church history, too, there have been many who have loved God's Word and found their delight in it. Here is what some of them said:

- John Calvin wrote: "Those only are worthy students" of the Bible who "are so delighted with its instruction as to account nothing more desirable or delicious than to make progress therein."

- "I was never out of my Bible," John Bunyan wrote. "Sin will keep you from this book, or this book will keep you from sin."

- "The longer you read the Bible, the more you will like it," wrote William Romaine. "It will grow sweeter and sweeter; and the more you get into the spirit of it, the more you will get into the spirit of Christ" (*Complete Gathered Gold*, 60–63).

- John Blanchard writes that the Bible "is meant to be a constant means of enlightenment, enrichment, and encouragement, its dynamic influence bringing a deepening joy in our daily lives" (*How to Enjoy Your Bible*, 8).

The reasons men and women have found so much joy in the Word are the same as the reasons for reading it in the first place. It is the Word of God. Those who love God love to hear from Him. They love to read the words He has given them. Those words are true and full of wisdom. What a pleasure to find truth and wisdom in a world so devoid of those things.

Besides these factors, there is another: the content of the Bible is simply remarkable. Sometimes those of us who have grown up in Christian homes lose sight of this. We've heard the stories so many times that we fail to see their striking beauty. The Bible contains an overarching narrative that stretches from creation to the end of the world and beyond. It is so intricate and so simple at the same time. It is full of stories of men and women, young people, and boys and girls; of great sin and of even greater grace. It contains letters, prophecies, fables, parables, commands, and promises. It's packed full of amazing things. On every page, there is beauty to be found. And it's all true. Oh, praise God for the Bible! It's beautiful and true. When you see this beauty, reading your Bible is such a delight. It's a joy unlike any other to delve into the living Word of the living God. What other book could compare? Reading it remains hard work and it still requires discipline, but it's joyful work and it's a discipline with great reward.

READING THE BIBLE IS WORTH THE EFFORT

We've seen that reading your Bible is one of the hardest things to do. You know it's hard work, but I hope you also see that it is totally worth the effort. There are so many reasons to read the Bible. It's the Word of God Himself! Though the task is sometimes difficult, you can take these simple steps to make that task easier and to help encourage yourself to read even when you don't feel like it. By the grace of God in Jesus Christ, you will find joy in that Word— a world of joy. So take the plan you've made for a special time, for a special place, and for systematic reading, and go, read your Bibles. It will be hard work, but it will be worth it.

SELECTED BIBLIOGRAPHY

Blanchard, John, comp. *The Complete Gathered Gold*, 58–63. Darlington, England: Evangelical Press, 2006.

Blanchard, John. *How to Enjoy Your Bible.* Darlington, England: Evangelical Press, 1984.

Sproul, R. C. *Knowing Scripture.* Downers Grove, Ill.: InterVarsity Press, 1977.

"10 Commandments of Bible Study: A Guide to Studying the Scriptures." Compiled by Faith Free Presbyterian Church, 1207 Haywood Road, Greenville, SC 29615.

Thomas, Geoffrey. *Reading the Bible.* Edinburgh: Banner of Truth Trust, 2008.

Watson, Thomas. *Heaven Taken by Storm*, 12–15. Morgan, Pa.: Soli Deo Gloria, 1994.